What Do

Bahá'ís

Believe?

© Ann Vickers
Published by Warwick Bahá'í Bookshop 2022
www.warwickbahaibookshop.co.uk
Printed in UK by Clintplan.
ISBN 978-1-9993486-7-0
All quotations are from the Bahá'í Writings.

Extracts from the Bahá'í Writings, compiled by the same author:
Inspiring Words for Daily Life
Short Selections from the Bahá'í Writings
Bahá'í Prayers for Everyday Use
Words of Peace

Short books of history, from the same publisher:
The Life of the Báb
The Life of Bahá'u'lláh
The Life of 'Abdu'l-Bahá
The Life of the Guardian
Three Heroic Followers of the Báb

Picture Credits:
© Bahá'í International Community: pages 5,13,19,23,27,29,31,35,41 and cover. © Ann Vickers page 7. © Shahram Yazdi p33.
From Unsplash: p37 Johannes Plenio.
From Wikimedia Commons: p15 PierreSelim, p17 Strobilomyces, p21 Godfrey Atima, p25 Clker-Free-Vector-Images CC0, P39 Daniel R. Strebe, p43 NASA.

This book is largely based on a series of leaflets produced by Warwick Bahá'í Bookshop. These leaflets were written by Paddy and Ann Vickers, with some contributions from others. Many thanks to them all.

Contents

Introduction – please read this first!

The Bahá'í Faith is an independent world religion which embraces all previous religions. It was founded by Bahá'u'lláh ("the Glory of God"), who lived in the nineteenth century. The Bahá'í Faith is basically very simple, but it is also very detailed – it has teachings on all aspects of life. Essentially it is about changing ourselves for the better and changing the world for the better.
There are three core teachings:

The Oneness of God: There is only one God, although He may be called by many different names.

The Oneness of Religion: God has sent His Messengers at different times and places in human history. No part of the world has been left out. Bahá'ís believe there is actually only one religion - the religion of God - and that each of these Messengers takes us a step further forward. Their spiritual teachings are basically the same but the social teachings are different because they suit the needs of the particular time in which they were revealed. Bahá'ís believe that Bahá'u'lláh is the most recent Messenger of God, bringing teachings that are meant for this age and for the whole world. There will be more Messengers in the future.

The Oneness of Humanity: The specific mission of Bahá'u'lláh is to bring unity, peace and justice to the world. This is the first time in history that world unity is a practical possibility. There are many Bahá'í principles which work towards this goal and these are explained in this book. These teachings were revolutionary at the time, and the world still hasn't caught up with most of them!

"The gift of God to this enlightened age is the knowledge of the oneness of mankind and of the fundamental oneness of religion."

This book is not long enough to cover everything so it concentrates on what is different and new, or explained in a new way. As already mentioned, the spiritual teachings are the same in every religion, but they may be expanded or clarified as time moves forward.

All the quotations used in this book are from the Bahá'í Writings. Bahá'u'lláh appointed His son, 'Abdu'l-Bahá ("Servant of Bahá") to explain and interpret His Writings where necessary. Therefore the words of 'Abdu'l-Bahá are also considered as Bahá'í scripture.

There is a short history of the Bahá'í Faith at the end of the book which explains the key figures and events.

For more information see the very end of the book.

What is God?

Bahá'ís believe that God created us and everything we see around us. If this is true, then it is impossible for us to really understand what God is, in the same way that a painting can't understand the person who painted it, nor a table understand the carpenter who designed and made it. But we could tell something about the carpenter by looking at the table. Is it beautifully and carefully made, or is it rough and not properly finished? If it is beautifully and carefully made, then we can assume that the carpenter is someone who appreciates beauty and is a careful person who takes a pride in his or her work. In the same way we can learn about God from His creation. *

We can see, from the world around us, how the lower levels of creation cannot understand those above. For instance, a rock cannot understand how it feels for a plant to grow. A plant cannot understand how it feels for an animal to be able to see and hear, and an animal cannot understand how a human being can imagine something and bring it into being. In the same way, a human being cannot understand the powers of God. Although all of these things exist in the same world at the same time, each level is unable to comprehend those above, or even imagine the powers they have.

So how then could we possibly imagine what God is like? We can only learn about Him through His creation and from His Messengers.

*Note: people usually refer to God as "He", but in reality God cannot be male or female. But using "It" instead of "He" would make God an object, not a living being. So Bahá'ís follow the convention of using "He" with a capital letter to show respect.

"Know thou that every created thing is a sign of the revelation of God."

Just because we can't see God, it doesn't mean that God doesn't exist. We can't see love, but we can feel its effects. We can't see electricity, but we can see its power when it produces light or heat or makes something move. In the same way, we can't see God, but we can experience His power and His love. God is the most perfect Being – the most loving, the most kind, the most generous.

Why are there Different Religions?

In each age God chooses someone to be a channel for His guidance to humanity. Bahá'ís use the term "Manifestation of God" to refer to these Prophets or Messengers, because they manifest (or show) God's qualities to us. Bahá'ís believe that, among others, Krishna, Moses, Buddha, Christ, Muhammad and Bahá'u'lláh were Manifestations of God.

Bahá'ís believe that there must have been many other Manifestations or Messengers in the past Who came for the populations of all the different parts of the world. This was before the age of writing so we don't know much about them. But traces of these can be found in local folklore in many parts of the world. God will never leave humanity without guidance.

The Messengers of God are like perfect mirrors reflecting the light of God. If we look at the sun reflected in a mirror, we can truthfully say that we have seen the sun. But the sun has not come down out of the sky into the mirror. So it is with the Manifestations: they are perfect mirrors in which we can see the beauty and goodness of God.

On the one hand these Messengers are human, like us, but on the other hand they are speaking as the voice of God. This is why a Messenger sometimes speaks as God, and sometimes as a human being. For example, at one time Jesus Christ said, *"I and my Father are one"* (John 10 v.30), and at another time He said, *"Why callest thou me good? There is none good but one, that is, God"* (Mark 10 v.18).

"... the essence of all the Prophets of God is one and the same. Their unity is absolute."

The light of God within each Messenger is the same. It is only the human being which is different. It is like when you put different coloured lampshades around the same light. Each one makes it look different, but it is still actually the same light inside.

Bahá'ís believe that religion progresses from one age to the next, as conditions change and mankind's spiritual capacity develops. In this sense all religions are one, in that they are all inspired by God and are part of His great plan for humanity. In the sense that they arise at different places and times they are, of course, quite separate. It is like the sun: it rises every day from a slightly different point, but we still recognise it as the same sun.

The Three Parts of Religion

All the different Messengers of God have taught the same truths –
to be honest, pure and kind, to love one another and to love God.
However, as humanity advances, each Messenger teaches us more
than the one before. It's a bit like going up into the next class at
school: for example, it is only because our first teacher tells us about
numbers that we can understand when our second teacher tells us
how to add up. It is the same with the Messengers. They build on
what has gone before and teach us how to be better and better
people. For example, over many centuries most of us have learned
how to accept and live in peace with people who live in our own
town and in our own country, now we all need to learn to do the
same with everyone in the world. Bahá'u'lláh said:
"The earth is but one country and mankind its citizens."

The second part of religion is about what happens in the physical
world and is altered according to the needs of the times. For
example, if we compare the laws of Moses, which were revealed to
a wandering people, with those of Christ, given in a later age and a
more settled time, we will see a practical difference. Moses taught
"an eye for an eye and a tooth for a tooth", as a simple and more
advanced approach to justice than was the custom of the time,
when a person who hurt someone else might well be killed in
revenge. However, as the rule of law was established and people
were living in cities and towns, Jesus was able to go beyond this
teaching when He urged people to, *"turn the other cheek"* and not
to take the law into their own hands.

Bahá'ís refer to this advancement in spiritual and practical laws as
"progressive revelation".

"All the Prophets of God proclaim the same Faith."

Love

Respect

Honesty

Patience

Kindness

Generosity

Trustworthiness

As for the third part of religion: as time goes by, people add things to religion which were never meant to be there. Rules and beliefs are added with no basis in the Holy Books. Ideas and theories become accepted traditions. These additions are the things which most often cause difficulty between religions or sects. When the next religion comes along, these things are swept away and forgotten.

The Promised One

Each Messenger is in one sense a "return" of those gone before. It is the qualities and perfections which have returned, not the physical atoms which make up the body. In the same way, a rose may flower every year, with the same beauty and sweet scent, but we realise that it is not actually the same rose, though we recognise it from the year before, and it has grown from the same bush.

All the Messengers of the past promised a great World Teacher who would bring a message for the whole world. Bahá'ís believe that Bahá'u'lláh was that World Teacher - the return of the spirit of Christ, of Muhammad, of Buddha and of all the other Messengers of God. *

Bahá'ís believe that Bahá'u'lláh came to bring peace to the world. The main message of the Bahá'í Faith is unity. This unity of all peoples is what is most needed in the world today. If we have unity then all other problems can be solved. We can then have peace between individuals and peace between nations.

Bahá'ís believe that humanity, as a whole, has been going through a growing-up process over the centuries. It is now going through the end of its difficult period of youth and is beginning to reach its age of maturity. This means it is now possible to accept one another and to live in peace.

* Bahá'ís believe that Bahá'u'lláh is the Prince of Peace promised to the Jews by Isaiah; to Christians He is Christ returned "in the glory of the Father"; to Shi'a Islam the return of the Imam Husayn; to Sunni Islam the descent of the "Spirit of God"; to the Hindus the reincarnation of Krishna; to the Buddhists the fifth Buddha (Maitreya, the Buddha of universal fellowship).

"The purpose of religion...is to establish unity...amongst the peoples of the world."

It is also the first time that we have been able to have one religion and one civilisation for the world. Before this age we didn't have instant world communications. We didn't even know that some other parts of the world existed! Now we can very quickly know what is happening everywhere.

Bahá'u'lláh promised that there would be more Messengers in the future, because God will always guide and help mankind. The next Messenger will come about a thousand years after Bahá'u'lláh, but right now we need to put His teachings into practice and bring peace and happiness to the world.

The Purpose of Life

Why are we here? What is life for? At some time in their lives, all human beings will ask themselves these questions. Bahá'u'lláh explained that life on this earth is a training ground, a matrix in which each soul can learn and develop.

This life is a reflection of the real spiritual life. Many things exist in this world so that we can understand the spiritual reality. For example, the sun shines its light on everyone and everything, gives us warmth and makes things grow. Without it, there would be no life at all on this earth. The sun can be seen as a symbol for God. This helps us to understand, for instance, that God's love shines upon everyone without exception - though we can shut ourselves away in the spiritual darkness if we choose. This love is what gives us life.

Every human being has a spiritual essence which we call a soul. This is the part of us which recognises goodness and wants to be better. The soul becomes connected with the body at the beginning of life, but the soul is not part of the body. The soul is like a light and the body is like a lampshade surrounding that source of light. The light shines through the lampshade but is not part of it. When the body dies, the soul separates from the body and continues to live in the spiritual world.

We can't see the spiritual world, but that doesn't mean it isn't there. There are lots of things we can't see, but we can feel their effects. For example, we can't see love, but we feel happy when we know someone loves us. Imagine a baby in the womb of its mother. It has its own complete world. It has no idea that this is enclosed within another, much bigger, world, even though it may sometimes feel the effects of this outer world.

"Man is, in reality, a spiritual being, and only when he lives in the spirit is he truly happy."

When the baby is born into this world, it realises how small and confining its old world was. It has much more room to grow and develop in this world. It's the same comparison between this world and the next world. The next world surrounds us in a way we can't even imagine, but when we reach the next world, we will realise the freedom we have from the restrictions of this small world. It will be like a bird being freed from a cage.

Developing the Soul

The baby, in the womb of its mother, is growing arms and legs which don't seem to be of much use. It can move them but it doesn't get anywhere. But, if the baby doesn't develop arms and legs properly, it will find life is more difficult when it is born into this world.

In the same way, we need to grow spiritual arms and legs while we are in this world, because we will need these when we get to the next world. These are the spiritual qualities, such as honesty, generosity, truthfulness and kindness.

So how do we develop these spiritual qualities? Every day, we have choices to make, difficulties to overcome, chances to improve ourselves. If someone is unkind to us, either we can be unkind back, or we can rise above it and show there is a better way. If we see someone struggling with something, we can offer to help or we can ignore it. If we find some money, we can keep it or we can try to find out who lost it. These are the simple things. We also have more difficult problems, like serious illness or losing someone we love. When things go wrong, we can get angry about it, or we can accept it, learn from it and grow stronger.

Tests and difficulties are necessary for our development and they happen for this reason. Of course, we can always bring suffering on ourselves by our own actions. This can be physical suffering, for example we can be greedy and make ourselves ill. Or it can be sadness or remorse caused by the way we have behaved or have treated others. The spiritual behaviour which comes from following the laws of God will free us from both these kinds of suffering.

"Tests are either stumbling-blocks or stepping-stones, just as we make them."

If we do not accept the problems which life presents us, and do not use them as means for our development, we will cause ourselves much unnecessary unhappiness. We are all born with different strengths and weaknesses and it is up to us how we use our strengths and overcome our weaknesses. This why we are here: to learn and grow as much as we can while we have the chance.

When we reach the next world, we will see how much progress we have made. If it's not very much, then we will realise how far away we are from God and from perfection, and this is what we think of as "hell". But if we have tried hard and done well, it will be like "heaven", because we are that much closer to God and to perfection. If we reach this state we can help bring progress in all the worlds of God.

Prayer and Meditation

An important way in which we can improve ourselves is through prayer and meditation. Prayer is like spiritual food. The body needs physical food in order to grow and be healthy. In the same way the soul needs spiritual food in order to be able to grow, to progress, to become more perfect, more like God. Prayer guides us to do the right thing, make the right decisions, follow the right path. It opens our hearts for the power of God to work through us.

Prayer is connection with God on a spiritual level. If a person has a love for God, then it is natural to want to connect with God, to praise God, to thank God for His love and care and to share our hopes and concerns.

People sometimes wonder why their prayers do not always seem to be answered. It is only later that we realise perhaps that the thing we wanted would not have been good for us, or that something much better has turned up instead. Or we find that we have learnt a lot from what has happened. If we have the faith to know that God provides what is best for us, then we will happily accept the answer, whatever it is.

When people pray together it brings them closer, as it helps us to realise that we are all in the same position, going through this world together. It makes us realise that we are all spiritual beings and therefore we are all connected in the spiritual world. It connects our hearts and makes us united and more loving. Bahá'ís organise regular prayer meetings for this reason.

"Meditation is the key for opening the doors of mysteries."

There are no priests in the Bahá'í Faith. Our spiritual life is our own responsibility. Bahá'u'lláh gave us three different prayers for daily use, so each day we can choose which one to say. Of course, we will usually want to say other prayers as well during the day.

Bahá'u'lláh said that we should read something from the Bahá'í scriptures every morning and evening and meditate on what we have read. In this way we will come to understand it more deeply and make it part of our lives.

When we meditate we open our minds to the world of the spirit and we can learn about things we knew nothing about before. If we meditate on the things of this world then we will learn about those, but if we meditate on the things of the spirit we will begin to understand the true nature of the universe and the real purpose of our lives.

Health and Healing

We should all look after our health. Good physical health helps our mental health and the powers of the mind. If we are healthy then we can help one another and play our part in making the world a better place.

'Abdu'l-Bahá explained that the physical cause of illness is when there is an imbalance in the different chemicals which the body needs. This can be put back into balance by eating particular foods. Until we understand this properly, we will still have to use medicines and drugs. But there are already many illnesses which we know are caused or made worse by a bad diet, such as heart disease, type 2 diabetes and at least some cancers.

Many studies have shown that a plant-based diet is best for the environment and for ourselves. 'Abdu'l-Bahá said that our natural food is that which grows out of the ground, and that, in the future, meat will no longer be eaten. This will be a gradual process, so Bahá'ís are not forbidden to eat meat.

If we eat simple foods and live a spiritual life it should help us to avoid many health problems. Purity and cleanliness in mind and body are necessary.

Following the laws of God keeps us safe from many diseases. Bahá'ís also avoid addictive drugs, including alcohol and tobacco. None of these improve our health or our spiritual progress - quite the opposite!

"In a large measure, happiness keeps our health whereas depression of spirit begets disease."

Our mental and spiritual health has a great impact on our physical health. 'Abdu'l-Bahá said that, to a large extent, happiness keeps us healthy whilst depression makes us ill. If we can be content with whatever life brings, then it will be easier to keep ourselves healthy. If illness is caused by sorrow, upset or stress, then a spiritual remedy, such as prayer, is the best cure. On the other hand, a broken leg is best healed by physical means!

Apart from praying for them, we can help someone who is sick by visiting them and cheering them up. Happiness is a great healer.

Education

Bahá'u'lláh taught, in the mid-19th century, that every child should receive an education, and that if the parents cannot afford it, then the cost falls on the community.

In cases where a choice has to be made, girls should be educated before boys, for these girls will one day be mothers, and the mother is the first teacher of the child.

To Bahá'ís, education is extremely important. The purpose of education is to fulfil the spiritual, intellectual, physical and practical potential of each individual. This will not only bring happiness to each person but will enable them to contribute to the general welfare of the world of humanity. Bahá'u'lláh said that each child is like a mine full of sparkling jewels. It is education which finds these jewels or talents and polishes them. Education is therefore about finding, encouraging and developing the talents of each child.

'Abdu'l-Bahá described three kinds of education: material, human and spiritual. Material education is to do with the body, improving health, food and so on. Human education is to do with civilisation and progress, for example, government, sciences, arts and trades. Spiritual education is concerned with developing virtues and perfections such as kindness, honesty and trustworthiness. All three kinds of education are necessary, but education in virtues and morals is the most important. If a child has a good character but doesn't know very much, that is better than if a child knows everything but behaves badly. But obviously if a child is knowledgeable and well-behaved, that is best of all!
Bahá'ís run children's classes (for all children) where virtues are taught and practised.

"Every child is potentially the light of the world..."

For older children and young teenagers there are junior youth groups which provide a space where they learn to think positively about themselves and about their contribution to the world.

One of the basic Bahá'í principles is that individuals should investigate truth for themselves. Bahá'í children are therefore encouraged to learn about different beliefs and to respect them. Bahá'ís teach their children to see themselves as world citizens so that prejudices of gender, race or nation will not appear.

Bahá'ís continue learning for the whole of their lives. One way of learning together is through study circles, which cover both spiritual matters and the concerns of the age in which we live. These are not just for Bahá'ís. They include learning how to run children's classes and junior youth groups and are open to everyone.

Science and Religion

It is one of the basic principles of the Bahá'í Faith that religion and science should be in harmony. They should work together for the improvement of the world. They are like the two wings of a bird. If we try to fly with the wing of religion alone, we will fall into superstition. If we try to fly with the wing of science alone, we will sink into materialism.

In recent centuries, there has been a certain amount of conflict between scientists and followers of religion. To a Bahá'í, this doesn't make sense. If science is discovered truth, then religion is revealed truth, so they should agree with one another. Each Messenger of God brings to humanity that which is needed to take society forward at that particular time. This spiritual energy brings forth new discoveries and inventions.

Bahá'ís believe that the universe has always existed in some form, but that it evolves from one state to another. Scientific theory has likewise concluded that the universe has no beginning, because the current "Big Bang" theory can only trace the history of the universe to a fraction of a second after the "Bang", and is not yet able to discover what form the universe took before this or why the "Bang" happened.

Bahá'ís believe that there have been human beings on this earth for a very long time, though they didn't always look as we do now. If we look at the human embryo, we can see the development of man as a species. From a tiny cell, it passes through various stages, sometimes it even has a tail. It does not really look like a human being at all in the early part of its development.

"Weigh carefully in the balance of reason and science everything that is presented to you as religion."

Bahá'ís believe that the Earth is not the only planet which has creatures. Bahá'u'lláh said that every star has its own planets, and every planet its own creatures, whose number no-one can possibly count.

As science makes new discoveries, the use of these discoveries needs to be guided by the moral principles which come from religion. If this happens, then our efforts will not go into more powerful or destructive weapons, but will be concentrated on areas which help mankind, such as health, nutrition, agriculture, climate and so on.

Unity

The most important goal of the Bahá'í Faith is unity. This doesn't mean that everyone has to be the same, quite the opposite! Bahá'ís often talk about "unity in diversity", meaning that we are all different but equal. The Bahá'í Writings say that we are like the different-coloured flowers in a garden – each one sets off the beauty of the others.

A major Bahá'í principle is that we should not have any prejudice against anyone. We may look different, sound different and behave differently, but we all have our own talents and qualities to contribute to the world. Everyone should be valued and have the same opportunities.

One thing which Bahá'ís should never do is to talk about other people behind their backs. This can only have a negative effect on everyone involved. We should always look at a person's good points and not think about ones which are not so good. No-one is perfect. We can only really improve ourselves and that is what we should be concentrating on!

The Bahá'í Writings specifically say that women and men are equal in the sight of God and should be treated so. There may be some things which women are more suited to than men, and vice versa, but in most things there is no difference at all.

The Bahá'í Writings also say that we should be friendly with people of all faiths and seek to understand their point of view. Religion should make people love one another - if it just causes trouble we would be better off without it.

"The diversity in the human family should be the cause of love and harmony, as it is in music where many different notes blend together in the making of a perfect chord."

Bahá'ís value local culture (for example, art, singing and dancing) and particularly encourage minority peoples to preserve and practise their culture.

Unity means that we should accept one another and work together to build a better world, starting with our own local communities. Bahá'ís are building communities where everyone is valued.

When people are united, then great things can be achieved.

How the Bahá'ís are Organised

The Bahá'í administration is essentially spiritual in nature, although practical in application. The local, national and world bodies are all elected to serve for a fixed term and the system is the same across the world.

In each area where there are enough Bahá'ís, a Local Spiritual Assembly is formed. Its first responsibility is to look after the local Bahá'í community, but its decisions should be taken for the good of the whole community and indeed the whole world. An annual election takes place for the nine members of the Assembly.

All Bahá'í elections take place without any form of electioneering. Each believer simply casts a vote by secret ballot for any nine adults from the local Bahá'í community, aided by prayer and meditation. Bahá'ís should vote for those people who have the best combination of spiritual qualities plus knowledge and experience. The nine people who receive the most votes become the members of the Local Spiritual Assembly.

Each year, Bahá'ís elect delegates for a National Convention, where a National Spiritual Assembly is elected for the whole country. This National Assembly consists of nine people. There are National Spiritual Assemblies serving almost every country in the world.

Every five years, the members of the various National Spiritual Assemblies elect the nine members of the Universal House of Justice, which is based in the Holy Land. Because conditions in the world are always changing, the Universal House of Justice needs to make laws or take action which is appropriate to the particular time. It can change its own laws but it cannot change the laws of Bahá'u'lláh.

Those elected should be *"the trusted ones of the Merciful among men"*.

In many countries there are also regional Bahá'í councils who assist the National Assemblies with the work in their own particular areas. These councils are elected by the members of the Local Spiritual Assemblies in the area. The Bahá'í administration is constantly developing as the Faith itself expands and develops. The Bahá'í administration is very adaptable, as long as the basic principles, laid down by Bahá'u'lláh, are not changed.

The Bahá'í system does produce institutions in which humble, honest and fair-minded people are elected. The Bahá'ís see this as a model for how the world will function in the future, and the Bahá'í administration itself as a system capable of serving the needs of the whole world.

Bahá'í Consultation

Bahá'ís have practical principles for consulting together and making good decisions. The goal of Bahá'í consultation at every level is to discover the best course of action to take for the well-being of all. This means everyone, not just those immediately affected or within the local area. To be able to consult successfully, the participants need to have certain qualities. The Bahá'í Writings say that they must have pure motives and want to serve humanity. In addition, they should be patient, humble, just and open-minded. People with all the above qualities will share the same goal – to reach the best decision for everyone.

Before starting the consultation the group will begin with prayers. During the consultation, if no way forward can be found, additional prayers will be said to produce a deeper unity and to resolve the difficulties.

All opinions must be listened to with respect and judged fairly. Each person should speak frankly, but with courtesy and moderation. The elected chairperson has the duty to ensure that everyone participates, that each opinion is listened to politely and is carefully considered on its merits. The chairperson also needs to ensure that no-one dominates or diverts the discussion.
Each idea must be offered to the group as a gift: it should not be identified in anyone's mind with the person who first suggested it. This means that the idea can be changed and developed, or even rejected, without anyone feeling hurt.

If the consultation has been successful, making a decision will probably prove to be the easiest part. It is likely also that it will be a unanimous decision. But if not, then a majority decision will be

"True consultation is spiritual conference in the attitude and atmosphere of love."

adopted. Most importantly, each member should respect the consulting body enough to carry out its decision confidently - even if he or she did not vote in favour of it. This unity brings immense benefits. If a decision is not supported, it will never be certain whether it was wrong in itself or whether it failed because of lack of support or even because people were working against it. When a decision is carried out wholeheartedly, however, it soon becomes obvious if the decision was a mistake and it can quickly be altered. This same whole-hearted support also means that the benefits of a correct decision will be felt immediately.

Using this system, much can be achieved in a short space of time. This method of consultation will produce great results as it becomes more widespread throughout the world.

Bahá'í Community Life

In the Bahá'í calendar, the year is divided into 19 months of 19 days each. In addition, there are 4 more days each year, which make it up to 365 days. These extra days are a special time for charity and giving of gifts. These increase to 5 days in a Bahá'í leap year.

On the first day of each Bahá'í month there is a meeting called a Feast, which is the main meeting of the Bahá'í community. All Bahá'ís should attend if they possibly can.

The Feast has three parts, which are all equally important.
The first part is the devotional part, when prayers and readings are said. This brings everybody together in a spiritual atmosphere.

The second part is the business part. This is where the Local Spiritual Assembly (see "How the Bahá'ís are Organised") tells the community about its plans. People ask questions and make suggestions and generally discuss what is going on. This is also where the local Treasurer tells everyone how much money is in the local Bahá'í Fund and how much is needed. Only Bahá'ís can give money to the Bahá'í Fund and all donations are confidential.

The third part of the Feast is the social part where everyone gets to know each other and shares food and drink. During this part there may be music, singing, dancing or playing games as well. It is a useful opportunity to get to know people, ready for when we come to vote for our Local Spiritual Assembly. Children and young people are always an important part of the Feast and may have their own programme.

"This Feast is held to foster comradeship and love, to call God to mind… and to encourage benevolent pursuits."

Depending on the size of the community, the Feast may be held in someone's home or in a hall or a Bahá'í centre.

Sometimes Bahá'ís hold special meetings called Unity Feasts. These are like the normal Feast but without the business part so that everyone can bring their friends and enjoy being together.

Bahá'ís also meet up regularly in smaller groups for devotional meetings, in order to pray and read the Writings together. Everyone is welcome, whether they are Bahá'ís or not.

Bahá'ís and their friends also get together in study circles where they study and discuss both spiritual and practical issues.

Building Communities

In many parts of the world, people have become more separated from one another. Especially in cities, people often don't even know their neighbours. The sense of community and mutual support has often been lost. Bahá'ís are trying to restore this sense of community.

Some of the activities mentioned in other sections help with this. One of these is getting people together to say prayers, whatever religion they happen to be. We are all praying to the same one God.

Study circles are another way of getting together and discussing both spiritual and more practical matters. Everyone learns to listen to one another's point of view and to discuss things calmly and sensibly without arguing or getting impatient.

In these study circles people can learn how to run children's classes where the aim is to teach children the virtues such as kindness, honesty and generosity. They can also learn how to run junior youth groups, which provide a space for the older ones where they can discuss the issues they face in growing up and discover their true identity.

Both children's classes and junior youth groups develop a sense of service to the community around them. Prayer meetings develop people's desire to serve, and study circles provide the training to serve in various ways, including the running of children's classes and junior youth groups. 'Abdu'l-Bahá said: *"Think ye at all times of rendering some service to every member of the human race."*

"Dedicate the precious days of your lives to the betterment of the world."

With a sense of service we ask ourselves – how can we help to make the world a better place? How can we help those around us? Bahá'ís seek to empower people to make a difference to their surroundings and to the people in their community, rather than waiting for someone else to do it. This has been highly successful in many parts of the world. Schools, clinics and community banks have been set up and there are projects to improve farming and the environment.

Smaller organised service projects, by children or adults or both, can be all kinds of things, depending on what is needed in the local area. It might be planting trees, cleaning up a river, collecting for a food bank or getting the local community together for a picnic.

Looking after the Earth

In the Bahá'í Writings there is much said about the relationship of humanity with our environment. Bahá'ís have an attitude of respect for the earth and all its creatures.

Bahá'ís see the whole of creation as an entity. Just as the human body is made up of lots of different parts which all work together and are dependent on each other, the whole world works in the same way, as indeed does the whole universe. Therefore we are all dependent on one another's existence for our own well-being.

One of the basic principles of the Bahá'í Faith is justice. We all have an equal right to the world's resources, and no-one has a right to more than his or her fair share. Bahá'ís see global warming, deforestation and pollution as fundamentally the results of a spiritual problem. Too many of us have been using more than we should of the world's resources. Bahá'ís believe that the material aspects of life need to be guided by spiritual principles so that we can all have a sustainable and happy life. If we understand that our purpose in life is to learn and grow spiritually, to become better people, then we will not feel the need for more and more material possessions in order to prove our worth, or to try to make ourselves happy. It is a sobering thought that the source of all our wealth is the ground which we tread beneath our feet.

The Bahá'í Writings state that agriculture is the world's most important industry – an obvious fact which often tends to be overlooked. The methods of agriculture, however, need to be such that an ecological balance is maintained.

"If carried to excess, civilisation will prove as prolific a source of evil as it had been of goodness when kept within the restraints of moderation."

If we upset the balance of nature we will only cause ourselves trouble. Human beings have a power which plants and animals do not have, the power to discover the secrets of nature. We therefore have the responsibility to use this power only in a positive way, to ensure that balance is maintained in the world.

The maintenance of a suitable environment for all living things is a global problem. Problems like climate change know no boundaries and the causes need to be tackled at a global level. Bahá'ís believe that in reality we need a form of world government to implement worldwide solutions. It must be able to manage the resources of the earth for the good of all.

A Fairer Economic System

There are many teachings on economics in the Bahá'í Faith. To gain a better understanding of these, the Bahá'í economic principles need to be seen in the light of general Bahá'í beliefs. The most fundamental beliefs are, firstly, that we should treat all people, of whatever country, faith, gender, ability or degree of wealth, as of equal value as a human being. Secondly, that this earth should be seen as if it were one country, with a world government, world economic system and a world civilisation.

The current economic system depends on people buying and using more and more things. This is not a sustainable system, nor is it good for the environment. Such materialism must give way to a more balanced view of the world, in which everyone has the right to a reasonable standard of living and in which resources can be conserved.

Bahá'ís believe that the following basic measures are necessary to bring economic justice:
- all trade barriers should be removed
- a common system of weights and measures should be adopted
- a world currency should be established
- interest rates should be set at a fair level

These measures would make trade easier between countries and remove many of the difficulties faced by less developed nations.

Another Bahá'í principle is that employees should receive a share of the profits of their company. This gives workers both a greater role and a greater interest in their employment.

*"The secrets of the whole economic question
are...concerned with the world of the heart and spirit."*

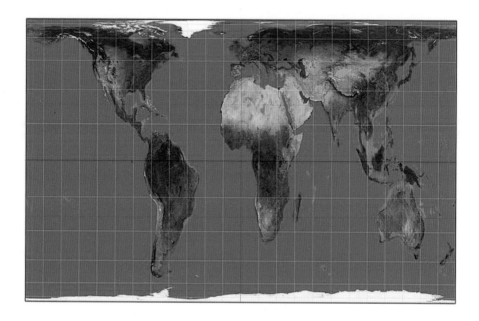

Bahá'u'lláh said that work, performed in a spirit of service, is equivalent to worshipping God. If we approach our work with an attitude of service, we are more likely to appreciate its value and to gain satisfaction from it.

Although absolute equality is not possible or practical, extremes of poverty and wealth must certainly be removed. Each person has the right to the basic necessities of life but no-one has the right to more wealth than he or she can use. There should be a minimum wage and the taxation laws should be designed to ensure that everyone exists within comfortable limits.

World Peace

Bahá'ís believe that world peace is an inevitable stage in the progress of humanity. If we do not reach it voluntarily, we are likely to be forced into it by disastrous circumstances. Bahá'ís believe that humanity as a whole has been gradually growing in maturity over thousands of years and is now reaching its stage of adulthood. This new maturity will gradually bring world peace.

In the 1860s Bahá'u'lláh wrote to the rulers of the world saying that there should be a world peace conference at which all the nations and peoples of the world should be represented. The object of this conference would be to agree a universal peace treaty which should:

* Fix the frontiers of each country so that there would be no more wars over nationhood or land ownership.

* Lay down the principles underlying the relationships between governments. In other words, how they should behave towards one another.

* Decide the level of armaments to be held by each country. This would be sufficient only for its own security and to maintain internal order. It would not therefore be a threat to any other country.

Bahá'u'lláh also clearly stated that if any government then broke this treaty, the entire world should unite to remove that government. This would mean that the world's population would be able to live in peace and security without the threat of war.

"Peace must first be established among individuals, until it leadeth in the end to peace among nations."

This kind of political peace is just a first step. We can then work towards a more positive and lasting peace, based on love, recognising that we are all human beings, all of equal worth. This is where we can all play our part, as individuals, in how we treat others. Achieving this kind of peace will be a more gradual process.

Bahá'ís have hope for the future. We may well go through some difficult times, but in the end we will definitely have a united and peaceful world where everyone can be happy, safe and content.

A World Civilisation

Bahá'ís believe that we will eventually develop a world civilisation, based on unity, peace and justice. This could more properly be described as a world commonwealth. Some elements of this have already been mentioned in the sections on Economics and on World Peace. Free trade and using the same currency and the same weights and measures would help to make it feel more like we are all part of the same one world community.

There should also be a world second language, using a single alphabet, taught in all the schools of the world. This might be a new language or one which already exists. A shared language would help so much in our understanding of one another.

A world government would make laws which are fair to everyone. It would ensure that the resources of the world are used sensibly and shared equitably. Being part of a federal system, each country would still run its own internal affairs.

A world court would make sure that justice is done and a world force would ensure that no country goes against these laws to take an unfair advantage.

When everyone is treated fairly, has adequate food and shelter, is able to live in peace and security and has equal opportunity to progress, and when everyone recognises that we are one humanity, depending on each other for our happiness, then we will have the nearest thing to heaven on earth.

"The earth is but one country, and mankind its citizens."

"So powerful is the light of unity that it can illuminate the whole earth."

A Brief History

The Báb

In the early years of the nineteenth century, many religious people were expecting something important to happen. Some Christians had worked out from the prophecies in the Bible that it was time for Christ to return. Some Muslims thought that it was time for the person promised by Muhammad to appear. In Iran there was a group of people who were travelling to different places, looking for the Promised One. On May 22nd 1844, one of these people met someone who claimed to be something special: He said that He had been sent by God to prepare the way for the Promised One of all religions. He called Himself the Báb, an Arabic word meaning the Door or Gate, to show that He was the gateway to the Promised One. Many people believed in Him and followed His teachings. They were called Bábís. However, just as in the time of Christ, the authorities saw the new religion as a threat to their power and tried to put a stop to it. Many thousands of Bábís were tortured and killed because of their beliefs. The Báb Himself was executed on July 9th 1850, but this did not stop His teachings from spreading.

Bahá'u'lláh

One of the Báb's followers was a man called Mirza Husayn Ali. He had the title Bahá'u'lláh, which means the Glory of God. This man was born into a wealthy and powerful family, but he was not interested in wealth or power. He was a very spiritual man who spent his time caring for others. He was known as "the Father of the Poor". When he heard the teachings of the Báb, he immediately became a believer. All of his possessions were taken from him, and, like many other Bábís, he was beaten and imprisoned for his faith. He was put into a dungeon in Teheran with a very heavy chain around his neck. It was so heavy that he could not sit upright. The dungeon was filthy, there was no light or fresh air. But the Bábís who were in that prison used to chant prayers together every night.

It was while he was there that Bahá'u'lláh came to realise that he was chosen by God to be the Promised One.

After a while, Bahá'u'lláh was released from prison. The authorities wanted to get rid of Him so, although He was very ill, He was immediately sent away to another country - to Baghdad in Iraq. Many Bábís followed Him there and He also attracted many new followers in the city. Eventually the authorities decided to send Him even further away. Before He went, Bahá'u'lláh stayed in a garden just outside the city. This place became known as the Garden of Ridván, or Paradise. There He announced that He was the Promised One of all religions. Many people had realised this already, but they were all overjoyed to hear the announcement. But they were also sad because Bahá'u'lláh was being sent away from them, on a long journey across to the far side of Turkey, before finally being sent to the city of Akká in the Holy Land.

The whole of the city of Akká was a prison, but Bahá'u'lláh, all His family and more than 70 of His followers, were imprisoned in two rooms within its fortress, and they all suffered very badly. After about two years they were moved to a house where they had a little more space. Gradually the authorities realised that Bahá'u'lláh was not a danger to anyone and He was allowed to go free. For the last few years of His life He lived just outside the city.

Bahá'u'lláh passed to the next world on May 29th 1892. He had sacrificed His whole life for the sake of God. He gave up His life of luxury and ease and devoted Himself to the service of mankind. His mission was to remind the world of the love of God, to tell of God's purpose for this age, that the time has come for the people of the world to live in peace together. During His long years of imprisonment, He wrote many books and letters. He wrote to the leaders of the world, telling them that they should not spend money on armaments while their people starved, but should work together to make peace.

Bahá'u'lláh was willing to spend most of His life as a prisoner so that everyone could be truly free. His life was filled with suffering so that everyone could find true happiness.

`Abdu'l-Bahá

Bahá'u'lláh's son, `Abdu'l-Bahá, was left to carry on his Father's work. The name `Abdu'l-Bahá means "Servant of Glory", meaning the servant of Bahá'u'lláh. Most of his life was spent as a prisoner with his Father but he was always happy and cheerful because his spirit was free. He spent his time in serving God and serving others. `Abdu'l-Bahá was eventually set free in 1908 and, although he was now old and not very strong, he travelled to Europe and to North America to tell everyone about his Father's message. In 1921 he passed away after a lifetime of selfless service. Bahá'u'lláh had described `Abdu'l-Bahá as a perfect example of how a Bahá'í should behave, and so Bahá'ís should try to follow the example set by 'Abdu'l-Bahá.

The Guardian and the Universal House of Justice

`Abdu'l-Bahá left a will in which he appointed his grandson to be the Guardian of the Bahá'í Faith, as it was not yet strong enough to look after itself. Under the guidance of the Guardian the Bahá'í Faith spread to most parts of the world. He passed away during a visit to London in 1957. The Bahá'ís carried on with his plans and in 1963 they elected a world council known as the Universal House of Justice. Bahá'u'lláh had described this council and what its duties and responsibilities should be and `Abdu'l-Bahá had explained how it should be elected. This body looks after the Bahá'ís and keeps the Bahá'í Faith united. The Faith continues to grow across the world.

For more general information see www.bahai.org
For more on the life of Bahá'u'lláh see www.bahaullah.org

Joining the Bahá'í Community

As already explained, everyone is welcome to join in Bahá'í activities, including prayer meetings, study circles, children's classes, junior youth groups, social gatherings and service projects.
However, if Bahá'í beliefs make sense to you, you may wish to join the Bahá'í community as a Bahá'í yourself. If you believe that Bahá'u'lláh is the Messenger of God for this age then you are a Bahá'í. The first step is to register this with the Bahá'í community.

You will then naturally wish to follow Bahá'u'lláh's advice and His laws, which Bahá'ís believe are the laws of God designed for this age.

Some of the personal laws have been mentioned already, such as praying every day, not talking about people behind their backs, and avoiding alcohol and other habit-forming drugs.

There are other laws for the whole world, most of which have been mentioned in this book, such as education for everyone, a world government and a world currency.

All of the laws are meant for our own good and for the good of everyone. They are all designed by God for our happiness and well-being – for our spiritual, mental and physical health.

Sometimes people think they need to be perfect before becoming a Bahá'í – if that were the case, there would be no Bahá'ís at all!
We are all trying to improve ourselves and the world around us. By becoming part of the Bahá'í community we are able to help and support one another along the way.
If you are not already in touch with Bahá'ís please see overleaf for contact details.

Finding Out More

If you need to know more before you decide whether Bahá'u'lláh is the Messenger of God for this age, then there are different ways you can do this.

The international Bahá'í website at www.bahai.org is a good starting point, giving a lot of general information.

If you are already in contact with Bahá'ís, that's great, then I'm sure they will be able to explain whatever else you need to know and lend you some more books to read if you wish. If not, then there are several ways you can get in touch.

You can use www.bahai.org/national-communities to find the website for the Bahá'í community in any country. This should give more information, plus other contact details such as a telephone number and an e-mail address or a contact form.

Some websites and phone numbers:

UK	www.bahai.org.uk	0207 584 2566
USA	www.bahai.us	1-800-22-UNITE
Canada	www.bahai.ca	+1(905) 889-8168
Australia	www.bahai.org.au	(02) 9998 9222

Bahá'í books are available to buy from online bookshops across the world, for example:
https://books.bahai.org.uk (UK)
www.bahaibookstore.com (USA)
https://bookstore.bahai.ca (Canada)
https://bahaibooks.com.au (Australia)

Good luck with your search!